EASY POP MELODIES

FOR FLUTE

T0071733

ISBN 978-1-4803-8428-6

HAL•LEONARD®
CORPORATION
7777 W. BLUEMOUND RD. P.O. BOX 13819 MILWAUKEE, WI 53213

Visit Hal Leonard Online at
www.halleonard.com

ALL MY LOVING

FLUTE

Words and Music by JOHN LENNON
and PAUL McCARTNEY

BEAUTY AND THE BEAST

from Walt Disney's BEAUTY AND THE BEAST

Flute

Lyrics by HOWARD ASHMAN
Music by ALAN MENKEN

BLOWIN' IN THE WIND

FLUTE

Words and Music by
BOB DYLAN

CAN YOU FEEL THE LOVE TONIGHT

from Walt Disney Pictures' THE LION KING

Flute

Music by ELTON JOHN
Lyrics by TIM RICE

CAN'T HELP FALLING IN LOVE

Flute

Words and Music by GEORGE DAVID WEISS,
HUGO PERETTI and LUIGI CREATORE

CLOCKS

Words and Music by GUY BERRYMAN,
JON BUCKLAND, WILL CHAMPION
and CHRIS MARTIN

FLUTE

DAYDREAM BELIEVER

flute

Words and Music by
JOHN STEWART

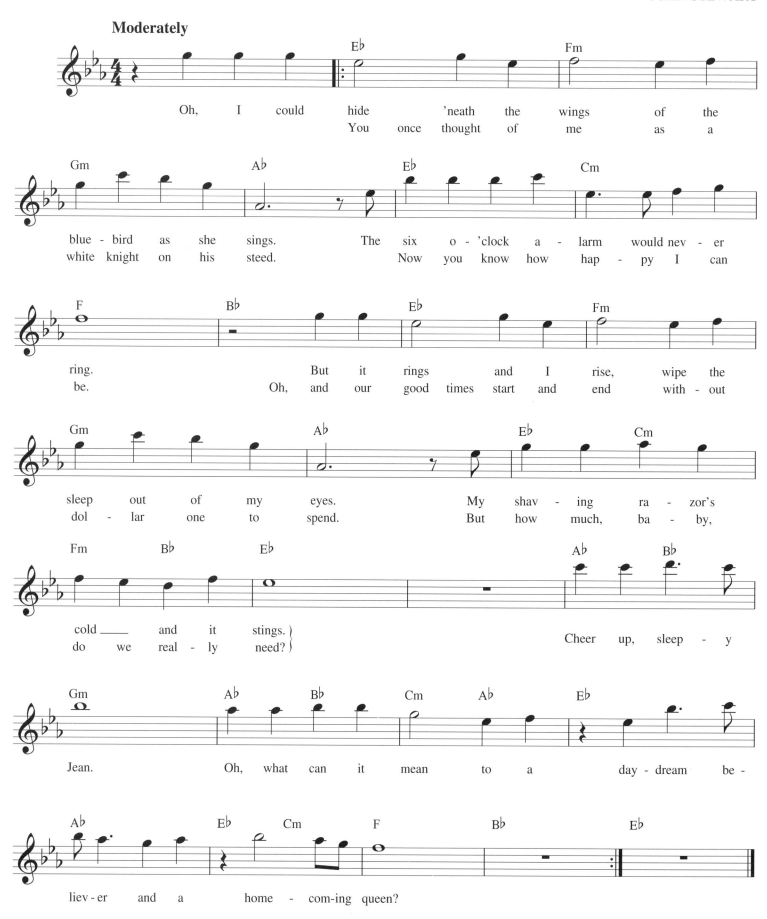

DON'T KNOW WHY

FLUTE

Words and Music by
JESSE HARRIS

DON'T STOP BELIEVIN'

FLUTE

Words and Music by STEVE PERRY,
NEAL SCHON and JONATHAN CAIN

EDELWEISS
from THE SOUND OF MUSIC

Flute

Lyrics by OSCAR HAMMERSTEIN II
Music by RICHARD RODGERS

EIGHT DAYS A WEEK

flute

Words and Music by JOHN LENNON
and PAUL McCARTNEY

EVERY BREATH YOU TAKE

FLUTE

Music and Lyrics by
STING

FIREFLIES

FLUTE

Words and Music by
ADAM YOUNG

Moderately fast

Lyrics line 1: You would not be - lieve your eyes if ten mil - lion fi - re - flies

Lyrics line 2: 'Cause I get a thou - sand hugs from ten thou - sand light - ning bugs

lit up the world as I fell a - sleep.

as they try to teach me how to dance.

'Cause they fill the o - pen air and leave tear - drops ev - 'ry - where. You'd think

A fox - trot, a - bove my head, a sock - hop be - neath my bed, a dis -

me rude, but I would just stand and stare.

- co ball is just hang - ing by a thread.

I'd like to make my - self be - lieve that plan - et Earth

turns slow - ly. It's

hard to say that I'd rath - er stay a - wake when I'm a - sleep 'cause

ev - 'ry - thing is nev - er as it seems.

1. F ... Eb

2. Bb seems.

GEORGIA ON MY MIND

flute

Words by STUART GORRELL
Music by HOAGY CARMICHAEL

IN MY LIFE

FLUTE

Words and Music by JOHN LENNON
and PAUL McCARTNEY

HEY, SOUL SISTER

Flute

Words and Music by PAT MONAHAN,
ESPEN LIND and AMUND BJORKLAND

HOT N COLD

FLUTE

Words and Music by KATY PERRY,
MAX MARTIN and LUKASZ GOTTWALD

ISN'T SHE LOVELY

Flute

Words and Music by
STEVIE WONDER

THE LETTER

Flute

Words and Music by
WAYNE CARSON THOMPSON

LIKE A VIRGIN

FLUTE

Words and Music by BILLY STEINBERG
and TOM KELLY

THE LOOK OF LOVE

from CASINO ROYALE

FLUTE

Words by HAL DAVID
Music by BURT BACHARACH

LOVE ME TENDER

FLUTE

Words and Music by ELVIS PRESLEY
and VERA MATSON

Moderately

F / G7 / C7

Love me ten - der, love me sweet; nev - er let me
Love me ten - der, love me long; take me to your

F / G7

go. You have made my life com - plete,
heart. For it's there that I be - long,

C7 / F / A7/E

and I love you so.
and we'll nev - er part. Love me ten - der,

Dm / F7/C / Bb / Bbm / F

love me true. All my dreams ful - fill.

D7 / G7 / 1. C7

For, my dar - ling, I love you, and I al - ways

F / 2. C7 / F

will. and I al - ways will.

MR. TAMBOURINE MAN

flute

Words and Music by
BOB DYLAN

Moderately fast

Hey, Mis- ter Tam- bou- rine Man, play a song for me. I'm not

sleep- y and there is no place I'm go- ing to.

Hey, Mis- ter Tam- bou- rine Man, play a song for me. In the

jin- gle jan- gle morn- ing I'll come fol - low- ing you. **Fine**

Though I know this eve- ning's em- pire has re- turned in- to my
wea- ri- ness a- maz- es me. I'm brand- ed on my

sand, van- ished from my hand, left me blind- ly here to
feet. I have no one to meet, and the an- cient emp- ty

stand but still not sleep- ing,   my
street's too dead for dream- ing.

1.   2.   **D.C. al Fine**

LOVE STORY

FLUTE

Words and Music by
TAYLOR SWIFT

MOON RIVER

from the Paramount Picture BREAKFAST AT TIFFANY'S

Flute

Words by JOHNNY MERCER
Music by HENRY MANCINI

MORNING HAS BROKEN

FLUTE

Words by ELEANOR FARJEON
Music by CAT STEVENS

MY CHERIE AMOUR

FLUTE

Words and Music by STEVIE WONDER,
SYLVIA MOY and HENRY COSBY

MY GIRL

flute

Words and Music by WILLIAM "SMOKEY" ROBINSON
and RONALD WHITE

MY FAVORITE THINGS

from THE SOUND OF MUSIC

Flute

Lyrics by OSCAR HAMMERSTEIN II
Music by RICHARD RODGERS

MY HEART WILL GO ON

(Love Theme from 'Titanic')

from the Paramount and Twentieth Century Fox Motion Picture TITANIC

Music by JAMES HORNER
Lyric by WILL JENNINGS

Flute

NIGHTS IN WHITE SATIN

flute

Words and Music by
JUSTIN HAYWARD

NOWHERE MAN

Flute

Words and Music by JOHN LENNON
and PAUL McCARTNEY

PUFF THE MAGIC DRAGON

FLUTE

Words and Music by LENNY LIPTON
and PETER YARROW

Moderately

Puff the Mag - ic Drag - on lived by the
Lit - tle Jack - ie Pa - per loved that ras - cal

sea and frol - icked in the au - tumn mist ___ in a
Puff and brought him strings and seal - ing wax ___ and

1.
land called Hon - a - lee. ___

2.
oth - er fan - cy

stuff. Oh! Puff the Mag - ic Drag - on

lived by the sea and frol - icked in the

au - tumn mist ___ in a land called Hon - a - lee. ___

2.
land called Hon - a - lee. ___

RAINDROPS KEEP FALLIN' ON MY HEAD

from BUTCH CASSIDY AND THE SUNDANCE KID

Flute

Lyric by HAL DAVID
Music by BURT BACHARACH

SCARBOROUGH FAIR/CANTICLE

flute

Arrangement and Original Counter Melody by PAUL SIMON
and ARTHUR GARFUNKEL

SOMEWHERE OUT THERE

from AN AMERICAN TAIL

FLUTE

Music by BARRY MANN and JAMES HORNER
Lyric by CYNTHIA WEIL

THE SOUND OF MUSIC
from THE SOUND OF MUSIC

FLUTE

Lyrics by OSCAR HAMMERSTEIN II
Music by RICHARD RODGERS

STRANGERS IN THE NIGHT

adapted from A MAN COULD GET KILLED

flute

Words by CHARLES SINGLETON and EDDIE SNYDER
Music by BERT KAEMPFERT

Moderately

Stran-gers in the night ex-chang-ing glanc-es, won-d'ring in the night what were the chanc-es

we'd be shar-ing love be-fore the night was through. ____

Some-thing in your eyes was so in-vit-ing, some-thing in your smile was so ex-cit-ing,

some-thing in my heart told me I must have you. ____

Stran-gers in the night, two lone-ly peo-ple, we were stran-gers in the night up to the mo-ment when we

said our first hel-lo. Lit-tle did we know love was just a glance a-way, a

warm em-brac-ing dance a-way. And ev-er since that night we've been to-geth-er, lov-ers at first sight

in love for-ev-er. It turned out so right for stran-gers in the night. ____

SUNSHINE ON MY SHOULDERS

Flute

Words by JOHN DENVER
Music by JOHN DENVER, MIKE TAYLOR
and DICK KNISS

Moderately

Sun - shine ___ on my shoul - ders ___ makes me hap - py.
Sun - shine ___ on the wa - ter ___ looks so love - ly.

Sun - shine ___ in my eyes can make me cry. ___
Sun - shine ___ al - most

al - ways ___ makes me high. ___

If I had a day that I could give you, ___ I'd
If I had a song that I could sing for you, ___ I'd

give to you ___ a day just like to - day. ___
sing a song ___ to

make you feel this way. ___

D.C. al Coda
(take repeat)

CODA

SWEET CAROLINE

flute

Words and Music by
NEIL DIAMOND

TILL THERE WAS YOU

from Meredith Willson's THE MUSIC MAN

Flute

By MEREDITH WILLSON

THE TIMES THEY ARE A-CHANGIN'

FLUTE

Words and Music by
BOB DYLAN

UNCHAINED MELODY

FLUTE

Lyric by HY ZARET
Music by ALEX NORTH

TOMORROW
from The Musical Production ANNIE

Flute

Lyric by MARTIN CHARNIN
Music by CHARLES STROUSE

VIVA LA VIDA

Words and Music by GUY BERRYMAN,
JON BUCKLAND, WILL CHAMPION
and CHRIS MARTIN

Flute

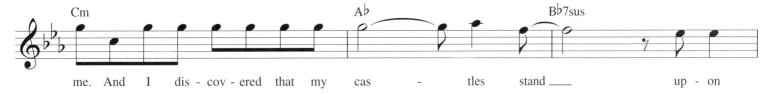

me. And I dis-cov-ered that my cas - tles stand _____ up - on

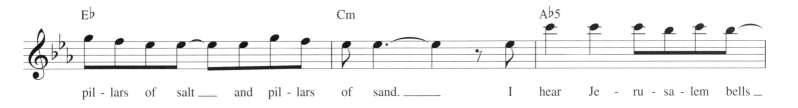

pil - lars of salt ___ and pil - lars of sand. _____ I hear Je - ru - sa - lem bells _

_____ a - ring - ing. Ro - man cav - al - ry choirs ___ are sing - ing.

Be my mir - ror, my sword ___ and shield, _____ my mis - sion - ar - ies in a for -

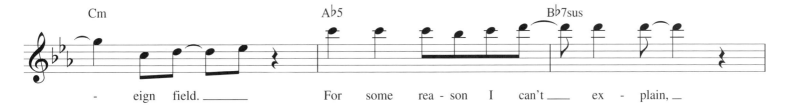

- eign field. _____ For some rea - son I can't ___ ex - plain, _

once you've gone there was nev - er, nev - er an hon - est word, _

_____ and that was when I ruled the world. __

WE ARE THE WORLD

FLUTE

Words and Music by LIONEL RICHIE
and MICHAEL JACKSON

WHAT A WONDERFUL WORLD

flute

Words and Music by GEORGE DAVID WEISS
and BOB THIELE

WONDERWALL

FLUTE

Words and Music by
NOEL GALLAGHER

61

YOU ARE THE SUNSHINE OF MY LIFE

flute

Words and Music by
STEVIE WONDER

You are the sun - shine of ___ my life. ___
You are the ap - ple of ___ my eye. ___

That's why I'll al - ways be ___ a - round. ___
For - ev - er you'll ___ stay in ___ my heart. ___

I feel like this ___ is the ___ be - gin - ning, ___

though I've loved you ___ for a thou - sand years. ___

And if I thought ___ our love ___ was end - ing, ___ I'd find ___

___ my - self ___ drown - ing in my ___ own tears. Whoa, ___ whoa. ___

YOU'VE GOT A FRIEND

flute

Words and Music by
CAROLE KING